MW01517806

VOTING TO WORK WITH MY CREATOR

DAILY IDEAS AND VIEWS ON HOW TO RELATE WITH YOUR
CREATOR TO MOVE TOWARDS WHO YOU WANT TO BE.

GERALD BARA

BALBOA.PRESS
A DIVISION OF HAY HOUSE

Balboa Press books may be ordered through booksellers or by contacting:

Balboa Press
A Division of Hay House
1663 Liberty Drive
Bloomington, IN 47403
www.balboapress.com
844-682-1282

Print information available on the last page.

ISBN: 979-8-7652-5913-9 (sc)
ISBN: 979-8-7652-5914-6 (e)

Balboa Press rev. date: 01/30/2025

My Creator is this wondrous Bigger Power that can make a big tree grow from a small seed. I find it amazing, and I have no idea how it happens every year. I ask myself the same kinds of questions about myself. Why do I grow or not grow to be who I want to be and how do I work with the Source of that growing itself? What works to strengthen my relationship willingly with My Creator; that which creates me and my life? The 365 views are an offering of how "Voting To Work With My Creator" can look like.

I use the word "Creator" or "Bigger Power" in the text below to refer to what is called God, Spirit, Higher Power, Universe, Life, Light, Source, Tao, Heaven, etc..

Ask yourself will the words be useful in
the tougher situations in my life?

Will you view the following words as something that Your Creator, Your Bigger Power wants for you.

I am able to love myself through the will of My Creator. When I go to love myself by myself I only get so far. I am a part of the Bigger Power that has the power to support me to totally love myself.

Asking for help from My Bigger Power will bring support where I am open to receive it.

Viewing the world of My Creator is viewing worlds that we are all a part of. What creates me is in them too.

Being worthy in my feelings of having my needs met will come when I work with My Creator.

Whatever is in the way of my growing experience of love, will to be turned over to My Creator. My fears say I am not worthy enough to have love somehow. Where my fears work hard to keep me from having love in my life, invite My Creator there.

Wouldn't it be great to experience more love in this world? 'Who' says my will is not a part of My Bigger Power. If this 'who' is wrong then my will has power.

My Creator please fill the vulnerable places inside of me, with light and love. Permitting My Creator to support my vulnerable places is doable.

Welcome the worthiness of My Creator to grow within me to be able to handle this world we live in with power and kindness.

My Creator views me having experiences of Love. I am created from My Creator which is the Source of Love, light and life. I am created from that same Source.

My Creator will reach into all parts of me to have me experience love within me. My Creator reaches into my mind, my body, my soul, my spirit, my sense of connection with My Creator and my sense of power to this world. My Creator works in all those places to work the pains out.

My experiences of happiness come from working to release my habitual programming that says I can't do it. We all have habitual programming that says we can't do it. It is not truly who we are or where we come from. Working through the negative habitual programming means voting every day to keep erasing that negative habitual programming even when it is viewed as weakness.

I have it in me to want love and light for others. It is tough to want love and light for all others. Some others I may not like too much. Withholding from others causes my body to contract. Which means less love or positive energy can get to me. And from me to those I really like and love.

I have it in me to will love and positive energy for others. My Creator is what actually offers the love and positive energy to others; what my part is, is wanting it to happen.

Welcoming thoughtlessness inside my mind sets things up for the slave and victim mindset to start to grow. Welcome My Creator into that thoughtlessness.

Releasing negative feelings from the body can feel like a war. Not reacting to negative feelings can be very stressful! Responding to our own negative feelings without showing negatively to others on the outside, is easier said than done.

Vulnerability can be a teaching partner supporting me to be successful. Vulnerability points out where I have fears. When I move through my fears I grow in my ability to powerfully respond to what is happening.

My Creator welcomes strength into my fear of love and positive energy. Fearing love and positive energy is a very human thing to do. But isn't it what we all really want to experience? Words like guilt, sadness, anger or anxiety name what is in the way of feeling love and positive energy. These demanding body sensations (Guilt, sadness, anger, anxiety) come up to be moved through to turn things around for the better.

Some people say changing is easy. The truth is changing can be a big deal at times. Remember to respect my own process of changing and what works best for me.

How good am I at welcoming myself in my daily life? We all bring gifts to this world. How much am I welcoming my gifts and then sharing them with others?

My Creator can get the best positive results within my life for me. My life would include my mind, my body, my soul, my spirit, my sense of connection, my sense of power, where I come from without my body and how I view this world. Welcome My Bigger Power to work within my life will work when I intend it to.

My Creator is welcomed into my life. It is my choice to work with My Creator or not.

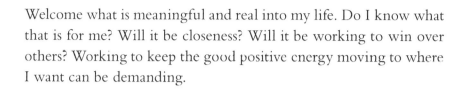

Welcome what is meaningful and real into my life. Do I know what that is for me? Will it be closeness? Will it be working to win over others? Working to keep the good positive energy moving to where I want can be demanding.

Welcoming all the qualities of positive energy for myself tells others what I can offer them. Qualities of positive energy, like compassion, mercy and forgiveness allow me to be a more powerful person.

To welcome what I want, which way do I turn? Will I Turn to My Creator? My own weaknesses would demand I turn towards what others say I want. Weaknesses would say they have "it" to give "it" to me. I just need to keep working them to give "it" to me. Moving through my fears will not get "it" for me my weaknesses would say.

Having faith in My Creator means asking My Creator for that faith.

I am able to calm down and realize My Creator is bigger than I am. Being able to trust that the power that creates me is bigger than me will make me able to do much more than I can by myself.

Welcome My Creator to show me the world I can live in, in working to experience what better worlds there are to live in. What is satisfying living really about? My Creator can show me where living can get so much better.

Victim voices inside me who have given up on living a good life will be worked out of their jobs by My Creator. Victim voices are negative views of what living is which we experience in our feelings and in our minds.

The feeling of weariness comes from drawing my feelings from weary places. Worthiness feelings will be drawn from our Bigger Power or My Creator. My Bigger Power or Creator is the Source of life, living, love and worthiness feelings themselves.

Situations unfold for the best when I offer love and positive energy towards them. Tough stuff happens in our life to point out to us where we need to grow in love. However, when we offer love and positive energy to a situation the situation is 'talked out' of negative feelings.

Welcome positive energy into our fear of loss. Weaknesses in us as humans make it hard for us to accept loss. When we go through a loss is a good time to welcome the support of Your Creator.

It is a good idea to permit My Creator to take what I have already lost so that My Creator can heal my pain. Where the pain of the loss is great vote to have My Bigger Power work love and positive energy into it.

My Creator wants good things for me. Wonderful feelings come from My Creator and I can welcome them into my life.

Worthless is the worst feeling to feel. The core view of what I am would be My Creator willing me to feel worthy. Working with My Creator to bring out the worthiness that is already within me will be my task.

Without me having to force My Creator to do so My Creator is already looking after me. When I have a need for something My Creator already knows it. Why do we all tend to think this is not true? My Creator is what creates me. Where I demand to get my needs met puts me in the way of getting what I really want.

My Creator welcomes my pains around when I view myself as having nothing of value to offer. When worthless feelings are working towards making me feel and think my life means nothing welcome My Bigger Power into those pains.

Generally when I run away from the good friends in my life is when my emotions are filled with "other people don't view me as voting to be kind" thoughts.

Asking for what I want is a lot tougher when love is missing. I am turning away from loving people working in my favor when I feel bad that they gave me good things.

It's time to vote to turn over negative views to My Creator when I stop viewing myself with compassion. I'm able to notice and become aware of when I start doing that. Otherwise living will continue to be tough.

Voting to turn over stressful demanding negative feelings through out the day works to help me feel better.

I find My Creator where I find the strength to over come tough times. Welcoming My Bigger Power welcomes that strength. At the time I am doing this I probably won't believe it will work.

Working towards becoming aware of my body sensations (feelings) is a working job that has great rewards. Asking myself what does my body feel like when I am Happy, sad, mad, guilty or anxious grows that awareness. Examples. Do I feel: Better or worse? Opening or closing? Light or heavy? Expanding or contracting? Shaky or calm? Tight or loose?

The uncomfortable feeling will be in my body. Is it in my stomach, chest, or throat? Breath into that area of the body 3 times and think "My Creator be in this area here too."

Staying aware of negative feelings means I need to remind myself to do it daily.

My Creator show me how to view myself with compassion when I ask for it.

I am able to permit others to get close to me. When I get closer to others, I enjoy life more and have more fun.

Working towards what I say I want works to move me towards the kind of person I want to be.

Feeling vulnerable will open me up to feeling some tough feelings. Feeling vulnerable without wanting to defend against feeling vulnerable moves the tough feelings through quicker.

Moving through negative feelings is easier when I will myself to stay within the uncomfortable sensation until it passes. As I get better at this I grow in maturity.

Moving through feelings is best done when I prepare myself to do so. Will I find my own ways to prepare myself? Asking other people how they do it helps.

The worst uncomfortable feelings tend to be unconscious. Keeping my self talk kind enough is tough when these uncomfortable feelings come up. I may find myself feeling bad for feeling bad. What helps me feel better is saying where I feel it in my body.

Take time to look after myself when I am moving through negative feelings. Engaging in humor, fitness, socializing and hobbies all help.

Viewing myself as someone who has value towards others will probably feel somewhat phoney at first. The negative feelings around this view won't move out on their own. The better feeling feelings are there to be felt when the negative feelings have been moved through.

Others may not know what to think of what I am willing myself to do. "Where-ever the will power to handle their negativity comes from, let me have it" is a good thought at a time like this. I may want to go calmly tell these people what I want from them the next time I do something they don't understand.

Feeling worthy comes from wanting to feel better. Worthiness is a choice we keep making through out the day even when it is tough.

Acting out my negative feelings on others won't bring me lasting good feelings. Willing myself to go move through the negative feelings brings the lasting good feelings.

Walking away from acting out my negative feelings on others will require effort. Getting myself to respond and kindly move through my negative feelings is worth the effort.

Willing myself to want to keep moving through my "stuff" comes from My Creator. Welcome it every day.

Whoever is the person(s)/animal I most trust to be there for me; keep them close.

When I think, "Yes I am smarter than these negative feelings" the feelings are walked away from. Thinking alone will not let go those negative feelings from my body. The help My Creator can give can. This power is available to me.

Working to become aware of what I am feeling requires patience. At times I may not really know if that uncomfortable feeling I am having is a sad, mad, scared or guilty.

Working to wreck havoc upon someone else who caused me pain comes from forcing worthlessness to fall upon them. Thinking if I make them feel worthless I will feel better doesn't work. Welcome my Bigger Power to support me choosing to contain those forceful impulses.

Volunteering to help someone else move through their negative feelings is wonderful. Trying to fix this person will make them work for your goals and not their own. It is supportive to walk beside them just like friends going on a walk. Show empathy for their pain. Allow them time to come up with their own good answers towards their situation.

Invite who I think is trustworthy into my life. They will show me by what they do if they are willing to be my friend. If they show by their actions they don't want to be my friend it is OK to let them go. I may need to move through feelings around letting a not so friendly friend go.

Real growth does not come from hanging onto friendships where I don't enjoy their company.

Allowing who I want into my life is my choice. When relationships get personal is when I allow myself and them to share thoughts and feelings about what is important to us and what we do and don't like.

When the time comes to welcome new people into my life, chose it.

Being friendly to some people can be tough. Be friendly for my sake. There will not be any negative thoughts and feelings to have to move through.

Choosing to be friendly works to attract friendly people to me.

When I grow it feels good.

Who likes to be the wrong one? When I am the wrong one, working at relating with others has stopped. I may think that they deserved what bad 'stuff' they got; That I had the right to give that bad 'stuff' to them. Who do I truly want to be in this situation? Invite My Creator into this 'worthlessness' show.

Viewing my pain with compassion and kindness will be some of the hardest work I will do in a lifetime. However, it will bring me an enormous amount of satisfaction.

Having fun will not come from negative peoples' negative words to you. Why do I have to appease their views of what makes for a good life? When they want to force their fearful views on me I can chose to not have them in my life.

"Won't you be my friend and do what I tell you to do even when you don't like it?" Views like the one just mentioned are not friendly.

Would someone dislike me for me being true to myself? Yes. Will I be able to be a friend to myself? Will I give myself worth while views of myself?

My Creator will always hold me in their heart. There will be love for me no matter where I find myself.

Wanting myself to be different from what I am works to put myself down. Viewing myself without compassion for my weaknesses will create negative feelings for myself and others. Move through the judgements I have on myself.

Working without views of myself that welcome mercy towards myself works to put myself down. The harder I am on myself without viewing where I am with some mercy, the more stress I will have in my life.

I can move towards the belief of "Yes I am who others would love." When I really feel that belief is when living becomes more enjoyable and relationships are more worthwhile.

I may find it hard to feel forgiveness for myself at times. The guilt I feel just won't let me feel good about myself. Other people may say I am innocent. However, saying 'I am innocent" to myself may bring about a negative reaction from myself. Feeling my innocence comes through welcoming My Creator, the Bigger Power to show it to me.

It is satisfying to welcome good people into my life. Who those good people are will depend upon what I am willing to allow myself to receive. The more willing I am for good people to show up in my life the more they will. Want the good for myself that My Bigger Power wants for me.

Working at the willingness to see things through is tough when my daily life doesn't feel so good. I may not think I can see this through. Would I be able to remember that My Bigger Power is a part of me at all times?

The accepting of support isn't easy for most of us. When I am living my life I tend to think it is all up to me to get things done. I am a part of life just like the My Bigger Power is. My Bigger Power is a part of my life.

Having a life that has nothing to do with My Creator will be lonely. My Creator will support my ability to welcome willing support into my life.

Wanting to make things better for myself and others shows others who I am. It's important to move through the thinking patterns that keep me from working to make things better.

Acting is supported by my choosing to move through my fears. When I move through my fears as best as I can I act more confidently.

When fears are running around my mind and body the worst results tend to happen. To get the best results wait until the negative stuff is moved through enough. I will act better when I am viewing what is going on from a less fearful mind and body.

Permit myself the right to want what I want for myself. Work for the right to follow up on that.

Would others judge my life as wrong? Point out to them that they will never have the right to be your judge.

Wanting to work towards something better shows others who I am. What that is, is up to me.

My Bigger Power can do much more than I can with my life. Willing that into my way of thinking may take some work.

When negative feelings are not moved through the worst things can happen. What happens tends to mirror what I dreaded would happen. My Bigger Power gives me as many chances as I need.

Viewing what is working and what isn't working in my life, must be one of the toughest things to do. How would My Bigger Power view my life? An infinite amount of compassion would be shown by My Bigger Power.

Do I chose what other people tend to chose? Do I chose what is comfortable? Do I chose what I feel will make things better? Do I view what I chose with worthiness in my feelings?

Trusting myself to know what to do doesn't always come naturally to us. Trusting My Bigger Power may not come naturally to us. Trusting humor to soothe my feelings will work when I use it.

Feelings of worthlessness would have me listening to others tell me how to live. This will cause me to doubt myself. What makes me think what I think is not good? Will I be able to know what to do all the times? How will I know what to do if I don't experience the results of my own choices.

It gets easier to live with "Yes I am human" over "Yes I am worthless." Moving through human feelings of unworthiness is something we all can learn. Willing myself to move through negative feelings I have had forever needs My Creators' help.

Walking away from being vulnerable will leave me feeling worthless. I am able to grow to move through vulnerable feelings. When I have moved through vulnerable feelings I find the good feelings I had walked away from.

People would say working through vulnerable feelings wasn't on my to do list for this lifetime. I do it because it makes me happier and more satisfied.

The views that My Bigger Power gave me on how I can move through vulnerable feelings works when I use them.

Trusting there will be calmer days ahead will not feel that calm at times. Worst days will happen if I don't move towards those calmer days.

Good times will come from letting go the tougher emotions. Being human has its good times. Being happy takes work at times.

Working to keep the pain away even though it always comes back will cause me more pain. Moving through the feelings even thought it is tough at times votes me towards better feelings.

Living with uncertainty can be demanding. I find the strength to move through this uncertainty working with My Bigger Power. My Bigger Power remembers me and knows what to do.

Where do I think I will be when I believe in thoughts that tear me down? Where will worry move me towards? Will it move me towards what I want? Turning those tear down thoughts over to My Bigger Power helps.

"Yes I will get out of the way so you can help me" is a way to ask My Bigger Power for help.

Is wanting MY Bigger Power to help a waste of time? Even though I still think that at times help will be given.

Would My Creator welcome my asking for help? Yes.

Wanting to view myself with more merciful eyes is a good idea. Where do I think that idea comes from?

Thoughts that tear me down come from fears that tell me life is tough and I will probably fail at being happy. Permit My Creator to work on my behalf to let go those fears will help.

Living in a world like this one is tough. When viewing others with kindness is met with distrust, mistrust may become what is expected. Would I be willing to permit goodwill for others even when it is not popular?

Living with kind people around us is what we all want. When I wonder where others lack of warmth comes from will I treat others with more kindness?

Do I welcome others into my 'world?' I may think my 'world' is better than their 'world.' Their 'world' and my 'world' both have vulnerabilities. When the two 'world's interact there is a sharing of where we both are vulnerable. We may call this dating for some people.

Dating is welcoming another's 'world' into my own. We get to find out what their 'world' is all about.

Determining when their 'world' will be good to my 'world' is what happens next when dating. A lot of deciding of where their strengths and weaknesses are goes on. Bottom line I find out they will not take on moving through my negative feelings for me.

When there is an honest sharing of what I am feeling without making it the other person's fault we will have a better time together. My negative feelings may have come up when we did something together. Doing what I can so I can control you so I don't have to move through my own feelings will not help the relationship work. Growing in strength to handle my own feelings will help the relationship grow.

It may be tough listening to the other person in the relationship express how they feel about something we did together without wanting to defend myself. Vulnerability will be hard not to defend. Negative emotions may come up when I lay give my vulnerability to my Bigger Power. The pains that want to be healed and let go will be in these big emotions that come up.

When I feel the negative feelings it is uncomfortable. It is very demanding to just breathe into the uncomfortable sensations until they go away on their on, without wanting to make them stop.

I will be pushed to my limits to move through my negative feelings at times. When I do move through my negative feelings it is very satisfying.

Being with someone being compassionate and responsive to my negative feelings can be even tougher at times. How can they feel love for me at a time when I don't feel love for me? Accepting My Bigger Power's support at moments like this won't be easy. When My Bigger Power is permitted in, My Bigger Power then responds to me and my negative feelings.

Choosing to be who I want to be in a relationship won't be easy at times. It will get harder if I don't.

Voicing what I do want and don't want simply won't happen over night. Pay attention to what am I thinking and feeling at the times when my weaknesses show themselves.

Wanting to stop myself from being vulnerable has a way of wearing me down. Worse things happen when I force myself to stop being vulnerable. Welcome My Bigger Power's support.

Controlling my vulnerabilities isn't possible. Working at being vulnerable with less and less fear moves me to feel closer to people.

Being vulnerable with less fear won't happen overnight. Taking the time to move through vulnerable feelings won't increase my paycheck. It will permit me to enjoy what I do with less struggle.

When living gets to be too demanding and expectations are 'stressing me out', the will to think of myself as trustworthy helps.

The will to think of myself as trustworthy supports me to increase working on saying what is right for me.

Viewing where I am as being able to feel worthy of success comes from My Bigger Power. There will be a lot of negative feelings in resistance to feeling those success feelings. Welcome My Bigger Power into the resistant feelings to release them.

Working through resistance to feeling worthy of success will require help. My Bigger Power can provide the help and attract good people to provide help.

Being the 'favorite one' of My Bigger Power will view myself as wanting to be as powerful as My Bigger Power. Truth is I do not feel worthy of being powerful. My Bigger Power offers the willingness to work power through out my life.

Feeling wonderful for being of real service to someone is me offering my power. Would I rather feel tough for having teared someone down and keep my worthless feelings?

Where do worthiness feelings come from? Where does love and positive energy come from? When I feel love will I be able to feel it without thinking I am not worthy of it? Worthiness feelings come from wanting to feel love and positive energy.

Viewing vulnerability with acceptance will show My Bigger Power that I am ready to live with more love and power.

Working with my negative feelings to move through them will make me feel better than working against my negative feelings to stuff them away.

Agreeing to feel worthiness feelings in my life will feel better than moving away from them.

Being around wonderful people in my life has its challenges. How do I feel worthy of those wonderful people being around me? Working the wonderful 'stuff' that is inside me, out to others will help.

Voicing the negative thoughts to myself and at myself comes first. Voicing the negative thoughts to others comes next. My Bigger Power can handle me voicing my negative thoughts. My Bigger Power can help me let the negative thoughts go.

My Bigger Power wills itself into my worst feelings to release them.

Working towards being vulnerable without being worked up and reacting means working with My Creator.

A strength and a willingness come from working towards what I love. When I move towards what I love that strength and willingness move too.

We all want what we want. Moving through the negative feelings that are in the way of what I want will get me what I want much quicker.

Being willing to move towards what I love gives me hope. Working towards that forward movement makes living feels easier.

It will be uncomfortable moving through the negative feelings. Walking away from negative feelings will be even more uncomfortable.

Being in charge of me brings me a sense of my own value. Have I been valuing the will to succeed or the will to be comfortable?

Do I think I will be able to win at getting my goals? I will be more likely to win with permitting support from My Creator.

Wanting to be true to who I am will bring up feelings of when I was not being true to myself. This is natural for any human. Letting go of what I think victorious results are supposed to look like is what My Creator does.

When worthlessness feelings are coming up to be moved through it can get tough. Trust myself that I can do it.

When I have a willingness to do so the worst feelings will be let go. The worst feelings will be released by My Creator even when I lack the ability to do so.

Living in a world that has thoughts that tear me down coming from my own mind is the worst world to live in.

Worthlessness feelings are not where I came from. Worthlessness feelings have a way of stopping me from moving forward.

The worst feelings come from handing over the 'reins to my life' to worthlessness feelings. Supporting myself until I can move through the worthlessness feelings works to allow me to keep 'holding onto the reins.'

The right to move towards what I want is given by My Creator. The moving maybe easy or hard or somewhere in between.

Walking towards what I want will require me to say what I want along the way. It can be tough to say what I want when my will to do so is in pain.

Forcing myself to be in charge of everyone including myself will not move me towards happiness. Willing myself to be in charge of moving through my feelings will move me towards happiness.

Wanting to stay in charge of everyone won't satisfy me.

Wanting to stay in charge of everyone and myself will weaken my ability to move towards the well being of others. Working like this I do not come across as trustworthy.

How do I trust other people when I have had my trust broken? Working through trust issues is best done with My Creator.

Trusting other people to treat me well may not come easy. When I feel good towards myself, then it is easier for me to set limits on what I will and won't accept.

The saying "good fences make good neighbors" has some truth to it. Keep my "fences" in good repair.

Being a good neighbor is challenging at times. Working through my negative feelings towards my neighbor supports to ease the tensions between us. When the tensions are calmed I can talk about where the 'fences' between us can be made better.

When willingness to move through my own negative feelings is worn down being kind becomes harder to do.

When I show others that who they are is bad and/or wrong they will want to do the same thing to me. No one likes to be the bad wrong one. Working towards a solution that you both can agree upon, even when it is tough, supports good friendships.

When negative emotions are involved it is NOT easy to follow up on how I'd like to be. Negative emotions pushed out at the other person or in at myself make it hard to be reasonable. Moving through my negative emotions is what is called for.

Working through my emotions can be very tough when there is something in me that wants revenge. Voting for a solution more than wanting revenge is much easier done with My Creator.

When revenge pushes its agenda vulnerability is very tough to permit to be there. Turn over the struggle between vulnerability and revenge to My Creator when I reach this point.

Turning over the struggle between vulnerability and revenge to My Creator can seem impossible. Vote for the right to view the situation with the "eyes" of My Creator.

Turning over revenge feelings supports worthwhile feelings to come back. What I turnover in revenge feelings I gain in worthwhile feelings.

Being what is good for me permits worthwhile feelings. Being what is good for me will support my good relationships with others.

Letting go guilt feelings will be the hardest thing I ever did. The guilt I thought that was weak and easy to move out has forceful blocks to my forward movement. Moving through these blocks is only done with My Creator.

Moving through walls of guilt feeling won't be easy when I am feeling vulnerable. Vulnerabilities want me to walk away from the guilt feelings. Being that vulnerable works to let go the guilt through My Creator.

Gifts given to me by My Creator will feel like a blessing and a curse. It is a curse when I withhold my gifts out of fear that the gift won't be good enough. My Creator helps me to let go those fears. Gifts feel good when offered without expectations of rewards.

Wanting rewards is so human. Rewards are rewarding. Not getting rewards can feel the worst. When I can move through my fears of not getting a reward then the rewards become moments of "Yes what I am is wanted."

Can I feel wanted for my gifts without the rewards? Can I only feel wanted for my gifts with the rewards? When I chose "Yes I am wanted for my gifts with rewards" I get fears following my gifts when I don't get the rewards. When I chose "Yes I am wanted for my gifts without the rewards" then My Creator can reward me with ALL the ways My Creator can reward me.

When living feels wonderful it is easy to offer my gifts. When living feels stressful giving my gifts can seem futile. It can be tough to feel satisfied when doing something tough. It is helpful to work through the stressful feelings.

Working through stressful feelings when I am already stressed seems futile. My Creator already knows I am stressed and feeling futile. Who would My Creator like me to be here? It is also tough to have faith in My Creator to help me be who I want to be.

Volunteering to have faith in My Creator can seem so useless to do. How do I know some helpful Bigger Power is there and will help me? Walking towards these doubts to move through them works to feel faith that something will be there for me.

Wanting to feel powerful is a common desire. Am I powerful enough to force others to give me what I want? Am I powerful enough to volunteer myself to work with others to satisfy both our needs?

Satisfying both our needs met has its' advantages. When my needs are satisfied yet their needs are not satisfied then our relationship will be stressful. Feelings of weakness come from satisfying my needs at the expense of others' needs not being satisfied.

Willing others to do what I want them to do comes from "I'm not good enough" feelings. These feelings say living is unfair so I must force others to give me what I want to survive. Work through these feelings with My Creator.

Living in fear of not getting my needs met will force me to push good people out of my life. Pushing good people out of my life works to get me to rethink what I am doing…possibly.

Working through something is probably not going to happen when the will to be in control voices itself loudly within me. When the will to be in control voices itself this loudly then I am under the control of feelings of worthlessness and will not be able to think straight.

Being under the control of feelings of worthlessness and unable to think straight is enough violence to get me to notice what I am doing…possibly.

Will power alone cannot move me out of these states of mind. Will power to permit My Creator into my mind is what is called for.

When my will power is weak then what is called for is the humility to be helped.

Trusting My Creator to help me out may seem impossible at this time. If all hope is gone what is left is the willingness to allow myself to feel worthless. Invite My Creator into the worthless feelings.

Worthlessness feelings feel awful. My Creator is what is called for at times like this.

Does my Soul stay with my body when I die? When I die, My Creator accepts me, my soul, home. Would I like to go home without all the negative feelings? I live in my body for now. I am my Soul forever.

Moving through negative feelings to be free of them in my Soul is for real.

When I welcome My Creator to hold my Soul in its' heart wonderful things happen.

My Creator validates my efforts for working my way home.

Permitting myself to feel vulnerable in the moment will feel very unnatural at first. Working against feeling vulnerable in the moment will feel worse.

Watch out for the thought that says "this is stupid" when working through vulnerable feelings. Feelings of worthlessness force that thought to happen.

Feelings of worthlessness will work to have me give up on myself. Moving through the worthlessness feelings when it feels the toughest is done with My Creator.

Will I be able to move through the worthlessness feelings? Harder still is the question, will I welcome the worthiness feelings in?

Being around someone else in pain can be uncomfortable. Nothing I can do helps to soothe their pain. Moving through my own demanding feelings at this same time helps to support them speak what they are feeling. When they don't have to look after my feelings they can look after their own.

When my feelings are demanding then expressing them with words, music, art, movement, etc. is supportive.

Demanding feelings will be tough to handle in my body. I can safely turn over the demanding feelings on my own.

Getting over negative feelings means moving through the negative feeling rather than working to will it away. Working to will away the negative feelings means holding onto the thought that says will power is more powerful than the feeling. My body can handle the sensation of the feelings even though my mind disagrees.

Moving through feelings will take my full attention. Viewing myself with kindness at these times is very important.

Welcoming the negative feelings into my attention so they can be moved through works to help me feel better. Not welcoming the negative feelings into my attention will work willful negative thoughts into my mind and body.

Feeling my negative feelings without mercy creates more negative feelings.

Getting mad at myself for feeling what I call 'weaker' feelings makes more 'weaker' feelings occur. We all feel every kind of feeling. Staying aware of feeling the feeling all the way through works to release it.

Feeling 'I am able to handle my feelings' is what I want.

The worthlessness feelings will be very tough to move through. Not moving through the worthlessness feelings will be tougher.

Experiencing demanding feelings without mercy puts the brakes on where I wanted the mercy to go.

The moving through my feelings is necessary. Keeping that in mind will make it easier to keep going when the moving through the feelings gets demanding.

When the moving through of negative feelings is demanding make time to go do what makes me feel better.

Working towards moving through the feelings at a pace that works for me won't be easy.

Working towards moving through the feelings at a pace that works for me shows I am capable of moving through my negative feelings. Willing myself to not work too hard or too easy supports the work.

Weaker feelings come from wanting to be some place where I am not. Feeling sad and expecting myself to be happy right away forces the sad feelings away from my help. Forcing away my sad feelings will work against my being happy.

Viewing my sad feelings as bad feelings stops them from being worked through.

Moving through sad feelings will finally permit me to feel the happy feelings.

My Creator's support is a sign of strength. Moving through negative feelings is doable when I welcome that strength.

Controlling the relationship with My Creator will weaken the connection to My Creator. Accept what My Creator has to offer.

Accept what My Creator has to offer to create change in my world. Wonderful change takes some time getting used to.

Moving towards what I want works to bring up helpless feelings to be moved through.

Viewing myself as able to handle this positive change isn't going to happen is what my worst fears would say.

Moving towards the letting go of negative views of what other people say I am worth comes from wanting to have views of myself that feel good.

"Why they are so bad thoughts" will limit my good feelings towards myself.

Relating to others in the worst ways comes out of my negative feelings. Either I think I am better than they are or I am worse than they are. I treat them better than me or worse than me.

I will lose feeling worthy of your friendship when I think I am better than you. Thinking I am better than you will make me not want to work at being friends with you. Making you do things I want becomes my priority.

Viewing myself as better than you will make me want to tear you down when you show me how good you are.

Victorious living for everyone works to have my life be victorious. This seems like an unbelievable idea. When enough people think supportive thoughts towards others, living victoriously will be the norm.

What I did in the past and have not changed won't move me forward in life. Voicing the right to change is not required. The right comes from being human. I must act if I want to change. Every feeling that says it won't work then comes up to be moved through.

My Creator strengthens my desire to move me forward. The process of moving through negative feelings can weaken that desire to do so.

My Bigger Power removes my worthless feelings with its' infinite power. All of that love and positive energy won't make me feel bad in any way.

Vulnerability will take its toll when I fight it. My Creator responds to what I fear to feel vulnerable about. My Creator works to weaken the fear of vulnerability.

My Bigger Power within where I feel vulnerable will make it a lot easier for me to move through my weaknesses.

Forcing myself towards willing vulnerabilities away tears down my ability to actually do it. Yelling at a mirror image of myself to stop yelling at myself doesn't work. Having mercy for myself for what I can't do yet is what my Bigger Power offers.

Walking away from vulnerabilities within my world weakens my abilities to respond positively to my world.

What do I do when others run away from their vulnerabilities? When a friend feels sacred of their vulnerabilities will I be able to notice and then reach out to them? Do I want someone to do that for me?

Moving through vulnerabilities as I experience them in my body works when I do it. Naming what the vulnerability is as I experience it in my body lessens the negative impact the vulnerability has on my being able to respond to it.

Without will power my trust in myself may go down. My Creator works as long as I put down my will that may be voting against My Creators' will.

Forcing My Creator into thinking that I know better does not work to make things better.

Forcing My Creator into giving me what I want weakens my ability to welcome what I want. Moving through my negative feelings around what I want and don't have yet, invites My Creator to offer me what I do want.

Working with My Bigger Power will be easier when there is a willingness to view taking from My Bigger Power with gratitude rather than a "you owe me" attitude.

Willing My Creator to want to help me will work to push away what I want.

When I feel weak and unable to follow up on who I want to be, tear down thoughts will be telling me I am no good. Will myself to work towards the vulnerability I am walking away from.

Vulnerability works to show me where weaknesses work against my success.

Forgiving myself for wanting to be in charge of the feelings of others will take some work. When others felt weak and vulnerable did I make worse their negative feelings by viewing them as stuck where they are?

Weaknesses show themselves without warning. View that moment with kindness with help from My Creator.

Will I be able to release what I think I know and learn what really works to make me happy?

Willing myself to want what others tell me to want works to make me feel bad.

What do I want to be able to work towards? What I want has got me in trouble before. When I work to make me happy when others disagree with what I want will make me happy.

Working towards what I want works to make me want to welcome new opportunities within my life.

My Creator wants me to want what I want. My Creator is telling me what to want.

Weaknesses show when I walk away from what I want.

Moving towards loneliness feelings to release their hold on me voluntarily is best done with My Bigger Power.

Worthwhile feelings come from moving through unworthiness feelings. Moving away from moving through unworthiness feelings weakens my ability to welcome good feelings.

Accepting tear down thoughts into my head will fight against the views that are supportive to myself and others.

Views that are supportive are views of life that are kind towards myself and others.

Being supportive to myself and others will be tough at times. My Creator works through my fears of being wanted by others.

My Creator weakens my resistance to being what I want to be.

Working to feel wanted by others starts with me working to want myself. My Bigger Power wants me to view myself as someone who is worthy of having company. Accepting My Bigger Power to be my company works to have me want to accept the company of others.

Weaknesses come from viewing My Bigger Power as weak. How will My Bigger Power show me they are powerful? Inviting the power of My Creator comes from moving through the weaknesses that say power is only given to those who are 'perfect' in the eyes of My Bigger Power.

Weaknesses come from wanting to be 'perfect' in the eyes of My Creator.

Living isn't meant to be what fearful people tell you it is. Disagreeing with people that view living with a closed heart takes courage.

Voicing a point of view says another point of view was in my decision making. The opposite point of view of what I want motivates me to be able to invite what works where I am.

Someone walking towards me willingly saying to me what I say to myself wouldn't feel very good.

Supporting a point of view means looking at myself to see if I am really supporting that point a view in my daily life.

A point of view will be easier to let go when I wonder how that point of view helps me in the first place. This point of view supports me to be the kind of person I want to be!

Voting weaknesses in my point of view comes from pushing towards a point of view which permits me to see others as less than human.

Inviting points of view will work to connect me with others. Weakening a person's belief in their point of view by tearing down their view of themselves weakens your point of view.

Voting to tear down their view of others for the sake of my point of view works to tear me down too. When living feels very tough I may choose to act this way. My Creator will comfort the pains I am going through.

Walking away from a welcome point of view to others wastes wondering how their point of view is good.

Worthlessness focused wills chose what suits their fears. Worthiness focused wills tend to chose what will make things better.

Choosing what makes things better will be choosing views that vote for other people to be happy too.

Finding the power to face worthless feelings in my body works when I walk towards My Creator.

Facing worthless feelings until those feelings move out will become a stronger skill as I welcome My Creator with everything I got. Saying how tough this can be moves the worthless feelings out quicker.

Being able to move the worthless feelings out quicker comes from wanting to wish it to happen with My Bigger Power.

Wanting My Creator to let me do this all by myself makes my will power weaker.

Wanting to work with My Creator is something that happens naturally. What I have done over my lifetime is will My Creator to let me do this myself.

Doing this work by myself turned me towards will power which did not work with the will power of My Bigger Power.

My Creator's will power works to strengthen my will power. Weakening my will power wastes my time.

Willful efforts by myself to get what I want work to weaken my will power. My Creators' will power along with my will power support me to get what would make me happy.

Worthiness feelings come from working with My Creators' will power. What that looks like I will not always know.

Vulnerable feelings come from thinking I can get what I want from my will power alone. WiII I vote to really allow My Creator to support my will power?

My Creator knows what I want to do with my will power. My Creator knows the best way to do it.

Trusting My Creator to offer me what I want can feel very unnatural. Working alone towards what I want even when I am never alone isn't natural.

How did I convince myself that I was alone all the time? Working with My Creator was what My Creator wanted all along.

When my will power works to pull others to what I want, weaknesses will start to show. Pulling others to what I want works to get people noticing I don't care about what they think.

Willingness to work vulnerable views will make it easier to say what I need to look at. Do I say what I don't like and do something about it? Do I look away from those things that make me feel uncomfortable?

Working to make things better even when it is uncomfortable supports living to get better.

Weaknesses come from not trusting myself to view my vote to do something as meaningful.

Weaknesses will grow bigger when they are not faced.

Willingly think of my weaknesses as why things are tough to do. Facing my weaknesses works better when I work with My Creator.

Working at making things better doesn't always go the way I want. I really need to relate with something bigger (My Bigger Power) which can support me to will things to go the way I want.

Working with My Bigger Power works when I move through my fears of my weaknesses holding me back. Support will be there even when I don't think I have earned the support.

Wills that lack power come from viewing other people as weak.

Wills that lack power come from forcing my will onto others.

People who force me to do things which cause me to feel weak view me as inferior.

My Creator is right there supporting me when ever I work towards what makes me smile.

Making myself happy along with making others' happy will make things better.

Actions towards what I will do to make myself happy will also make other people happy.

My Creator welcomes me to view what I am as a human being without wanting to judge it as useless. What I am as a human being will make for lots of good feelings.

Working with My Creator to decide upon a goal which makes me happy will get me to pick the best goals for me.

Turn towards My Bigger Power even more when the results I'm getting for my goal won't satisfy me.

Move through even more of my fears of My Creator loving me where I am at in my world.

My Creator offers me the love that is needed for where I am at. Will I receive it? Receiving the love of My Creator means I can't keep pretending to view myself as worthless.

Viewing myself as worthless works to create weaknesses within my character. My Creator views me as worthy.

What I would most want to give to others I want to be close to. (This includes people, animals, nature and My Creator). What I most want to give are the working worthiness feelings.

Choosing to view myself as worthy of love works to bring out the parts of me which don't believe I'm worthy of love. The parts of me which don't believe I'm worthy of love are ready for love.

My Creator creates me and all life from what it has. What it has is love.

Thinking of myself as loveable may feel very unnatural at first. My whole life up until now may have been filled with views of myself, others and life which have been negative.

Moving so much negativity out of my life will not seem possible. Waking up to My Creator moving the negativity out of my life will get easier.

Will I turn to My Creator when I think I can't do it? My Creator accepts my pains with every breath.

Will I vote for my own freedom from my own pains even when it is demanding? Permit My Bigger Power to chose for me.

Working to feel worthy but viewing myself as working alone works to create weaknesses.

Trusting My Creator to be there for me won't be easy at times. My faith in My Creator will be stretched to breaking points.

The breaking points will be the times when My Bigger Power will reach into me the deepest to let go the worthlessness pains the most.

Working with My Creator in my life does not happen overnight. What I would want to believe in can take time. (This process is like watching a plant grow).

When something happens I don't like do I move through my negative feelings? Working to control how everyone acts so I don't have to move through my negative feelings will push people away.

Thinking that others are the cause of my negative feelings will cause me to push for what worth I can get from others.

Thinking of myself as able to move through my negative feelings will support me to walk away from negative situations in which vulnerable feelings are disrespected.

When willing wonderful feelings for myself and others works, what happens is living becomes what I want it to be.

Violence is what it feels like when negative feelings build up in our bodies. Hanging onto all these negative feelings in our bodies without letting them go will create big stresses in the body.

Negative feelings in our bodies tend to work to weaken our resolve to want to view our lives with hope that things will get better. My Creator supports my will to hope until I can hope on my own again.

My Bigger Power has a way of reaching my hopelessness inside my fearful thoughts. The fearful thoughts won't be permitted to continue without love being added to them.

A world where voices of hopefulness matters works to make a better world.

Feeling feelings of hopelessness willingly to move through them may be one of the toughest things to do as a human being.

Moving through feelings of hopelessness works when My Bigger Power is involved.

Moving through hopelessness alone causes me to view living in ways that are vicious towards myself and others.

My Creator lets go my feelings of hopelessness when I don't push on My Creator to get it done.

My Bigger Power is willing to let go my feelings of hopelessness when I want peace more than will power over hopelessness.

When I want peace more that will power over hopelessness what happens is peace will move into my hopelessness.

Willing myself to welcome views of what is valuable compared with what other people say is valuable works to create a lot of stress.

We are not meant to view ourselves as less than other people. My Creator never intended that to be.

Voting for why others are lacking in goodness will welcome negative feelings into my heart.

Wanting to be what others want me to be works towards walking away from being what My Bigger Power wants me to be.

My Bigger Power works with me to give and receive love from each other.

When living starts to get easier it means I am moving through the fears I have of thinking of myself as My Creator thinks of me; with unconditional love.

My Bigger Power works to welcome other people working with their Bigger Power into my life. What that relating looks like will be up to us.

Wonderful results come from working with My Creator. Results which may or may not be good come from me alone.

Trusting myself to trust My Creator works when I vote to do so.

My Bigger Power welcomes my will to receive all this support from My Bigger Power.

Thinking of worthlessness feelings as something that can be moved through gives me the ability to want what I want instead of what I am supposed to want.

Planning will not always include what My Creator would have me do.

When the time comes to move through the fears which way will I chose? Do I Vote to work with my plan or My Creator's plan?

My Creator will vote to slow down viewing myself as already being there with my goals. What this does is allow me time to move through the negative feelings that are still in the way of my goals.

Welcome My Bigger Power into my willingness that might sabotage what is working well.

Working with My Bigger Power by my side will get easier as I welcome trust of my Bigger Power day by day.

Being willing to want to have more worthiness feelings votes towards wanting to love myself more.

Voting to accept love where I want to have better feelings works.

What My Creator does for me works to give me confidence that I can move through worthless feelings.

Accepting My Bigger Power's support with being willing to move through worthless feelings will grow.

My Creator votes for me to have worthiness feelings when I decide to vote for me having my own worthiness feelings.

Planning to vote for my own worthiness feelings is best supported by voting to accept the support of My Bigger Power.

When there is enough willingness on my part worthiness feelings will be welcomed through My Creator.

Trusting My Creator to welcome feelings of worthiness for me won't be easy a lot of the time. Worthlessness feelings may have been with me my whole life.

Working with My Bigger Power will get easier when I welcome worthiness feelings viewed as natural and willingly given by My Bigger Power.

Feelings of worthiness come from working towards what I look for in a voice that would come from My Creator.

My Creator offers worthiness feelings to me more and more.

Worthiness feelings come from working with My Creator without wanting to weaken others in any way.

Vindicating my success as something that can be wonderful for everyone will make me want to have even more success.

Leaving worthless feelings behind will become more and more natural.

Others do what they can to force me to continue to participate in the worthless feelings. Wish them well and walk away.

Willing myself to want to change for the better works to let worthless feelings go.

Welcome My Creator into my plans for change.

Vote to permit myself to welcome My Bigger Power throughout my life.

Vulnerability works it's way into my world when My Creator is not worked with.

Walking away from vindicating other points of view means I don't get to know more about what I don't agree with.

Walking away from worthless feelings will cause me even more suffering.

Worst feelings happen more when worst feelings have not been moved through.

My Creator works through my negative feelings with me not for me.

Wonderful feelings happen when moving through my negative feelings is done with My Creator, My Bigger Power.

Walking away from moving through our negative worthless feelings is something we all will do.

When it is time to commit yourself to doing this work you may want a coach to walk with you on your way. When that time is now I may be of service. What I offer you is views into where you may not be believing the 365 views. It is hard to be aware of where the suffering is. (Examples: Mind, body, soul, spirit, sense of power, sense of connection, our relationship with the bigger world) Awareness votes much more power into the moving through of negative feelings. My contact information is:

Gerald Bara. R.S.W. / B.ED.

Linktr.ee/PositiveResponseCoach
Email: Movethroughit@shaw.ca